— THE UNTOLD STORY OF —
BARBARA ROSE JOHNS

SCHOOL STRIKE ACTIVIST

BY NICOLE A. MANSFIELD

CAPSTONE PRESS
a capstone imprint

Published by Capstone Press, an imprint of Capstone
1710 Roe Crest Drive, North Mankato, Minnesota 56003
capstonepub.com

**Library of Congress Cataloging-in-Publication Data is available on
the Library of Congress website.**

ISBN: 9781669016106 (hardcover)
ISBN: 9781669016052 (paperback)
ISBN: 9781669016069 (ebook PDF)

Summary: Most people have heard about the historic school desegregation case
Brown v. Board of Education. That Supreme Court case actually combined five cases
challenging school segregation, and one of them began with a strike organized by
16-year-old Barbara Rose Johns. Uncover Johns's story and how the strike she led
helped bring about the Supreme Court case.

Editorial Credits
Editor: Ericka Smith; Designer: Kayla Rossow; Media Researcher: Svetlana Zhurkin;
Production Specialist: Katy LaVigne

Image Credits
Alamy: Everett Collection Historical, 19; Courtesy of Barbara Rose Johns' Family:
cover, 5; Dreamstime: Lucy Clark, 29; The Farmville Herald, March 20, 1951, and
The Library of Virginia: 13; Getty Images: Bettmann, 18, Pham Le Huong Son, 25,
PhotoStock-Israel/Cultura Exclusive, 7; Library of Congress: Thomas J. O'Halloran,
26; National Archives and Records Administration: Records of District Courts of
the United States, 8, 9, 10, 15, 17; Newscom: akg-images, 23; Shutterstock Premier:
The LIFE Picture Collection/Hank Walker, 21; Shutterstock: APN Photography,
27, Julia Khimich (background), cover (right) and throughout, Nadegda Rozova
(background), cover (left) and throughout; Wikimedia: William T. Ziglar, Jr., 28

Direct Quotations
Page 11, from May 8, 2019, *New York Times* article, "Overlooked No More: Barbara
Johns, Who Defied Segregation in Schools," nytimes.com
Page 24, from Howard University School of Law's web page, "Davis v. County School
Board (E.D. Virginia 1952)," law.howard.edu

All internet sites appearing in back matter were available and accurate when
this book was sent to press.

Printed and bound in China. 5379

TABLE OF CONTENTS

Words in **bold** are in the glossary.

A YOUNG WOMAN ON A BIG MISSION

Barbara Rose Johns was a young **activist** of vision, bravery, and determination. In 1951, at the age of 16, she organized a **strike** against her high school in Farmville, Virginia. Johns and hundreds of Black students protested the terrible conditions of their school—Robert Russa Moton High School.

The strike that Johns organized eventually led to a lawsuit against the school district. And that lawsuit made it all the way to the United States Supreme Court as part of the historic 1954 *Brown v. Board of Education* case.

You've probably read about *Brown v. Board of Education*. But Black people were challenging **segregation** in schools across the country. This is the story of one of the students who took up this challenge and helped build that historic desegregation case—Barbara Rose Johns.

CHAPTER ONE

NOT FAIR IS NOT OK

Barbara Rose Johns was born on March 6, 1935, in New York City. She was the oldest of five children. During World War II, her family left New York City. They moved back to their hometown of Darlington Heights, Virginia—just a few miles outside of Farmville. There, her father worked on a farm, where the family also lived. Her mother worked for the U.S. Navy in Washington, DC.

Johns was very close to her family, especially her uncle Vernon. Vernon Johns was a civil rights activist. He was also the pastor at Dexter Avenue Baptist Church in Montgomery, Alabama, in the late 1940s and the early 1950s. Vernon was outspoken about how unfair the laws in the U.S. were to Black people. He taught Barbara and her siblings to speak out against **racism**.

Dexter Avenue Baptist Church

When Johns was a student, all of the schools in Prince Edward County—where Farmville is located—were segregated. The white schools had buildings, buses, and textbooks that were in good condition. The Black schools' buildings, buses, and textbooks were in terrible condition.

Farmville High School, a high school for white students, around 1951

Moton High School around 1951

As a student at Moton High School, Johns grew more and more frustrated by this inequality. Moton High School had been built for only 180 students, but had about 450 students. School leaders had built shabby buildings to help create space for students. But inside it was hard for students to stay warm when it was cold and dry when it was rainy. Classes were also held in the auditorium and on buses.

Moton High School was missing some important facilities too. The school didn't have a cafeteria. It didn't have **laboratories** for science classes. And it didn't have a gym.

Students in a science lab at Farmville High School

In the fall of 1950, Johns was running late for school. She missed the crowded bus she usually took. While trying to find another ride to school, she watched the bus for the white high school pass by. It was only half full.

This incident encouraged Johns to act. "Right then and there, I decided that indeed something had to be done about this inequality," she wrote in her diary. Soon after, she came up with the idea for a strike and began to plan it.

An Unequal Curriculum Too

Students at Moton High School didn't have as many choices about what they learned either. They were offered fewer challenging courses. The white students in the area could take classes such as trigonometry, physics, geography, world history, and Latin. The Black students at Moton could not.

CHAPTER TWO

A TERRIBLE CRASH

On March 13, 1951, a bus for Moton High School was involved in an accident. The bus was a run-down hand-me-down from the white school across town. That foggy day the bus stalled on the train tracks. A train hit it—**severing** the rear of the bus. Five students were killed—Hettie Dungee, Christine Hendricks, Dodson Hendricks, Naomi Hendricks, and Winfield Page.

This tragedy highlighted the inequality between Black and white schools in the county. The local Black community was brokenhearted— and angry.

People gathered near the site of the bus crash just a few minutes after the accident happened.

STRIKE!

By the time the bus accident happened, 16-year-old Johns had been planning a strike for months. Secretly, she had been meeting with a few students to organize it. About a month after the bus accident, on April 23, 1951, they carried out their plan.

First, the students convinced the principal to leave the school. A student called the school pretending to be a businessman. He asked the principal to come downtown to help with Moton students who were there causing trouble.

Then, the organizers passed out a note to teachers that appeared to be from the principal. The note asked them to bring their students to the auditorium.

Once the students were in the auditorium, the organizers asked the teachers to leave. Johns spoke to the students. She asked them to take a stand and walk out of school that day. Most students joined the strike.

Students in the auditorium at Moton High School around 1951

Some students tried to meet with the **superintendent**, Thomas J. McIlwaine, that day but couldn't. He met with the students the next day and urged them to return to school. They didn't.

The strike lasted for two weeks. But it didn't convince the school district's leaders to make any significant changes. This only encouraged Johns and the other students to press on. If the school district wouldn't make changes, they were prepared to call on people who would!

FACT The students created signs for their strike that read, "Down with tar-paper shacks" and "We want a new school or none at all."

A classroom in a temporary building at Moton High School

CHAPTER FOUR

A CALL FOR HELP

The students reached out to lawyers Oliver Hill and Spottswood Robinson for help. Hill and Robinson worked with the National Association for the Advancement of Colored People (NAACP). Just two days after the strike began, on April 25, 1951, Hill and Robinson arrived in Farmville. They met with the students and with their parents.

The NAACP agreed to help the students. But they didn't want to just get them a new school building. The NAACP lawyers insisted on a different goal—they wanted to fight for an **integrated** school.

Spottswood Robinson (left) and Oliver Hill

The NAACP

The NAACP, founded in 1909, fights for equal rights for Black people. Their goal is to end racism. They do that in several ways, but an important part of their work is fighting legal battles. One of their most well-known cases is the 1954 *Brown v. Board of Education* case.

Young members of the NAACP protesting in 1940

After the NAACP agreed to help, the students decided to call off the strike. They returned to Moton High School on May 7, 1951.

On May 23, the NAACP attorneys filed a lawsuit against the school board in the federal district court of Richmond, Virginia. They wanted the judges to strike down Virginia's law segregating schools. The case represented 117 Moton High School students. The first student listed was Dorothy E. Davis, so the case was called *Davis v. County School Board of Prince Edward County.*

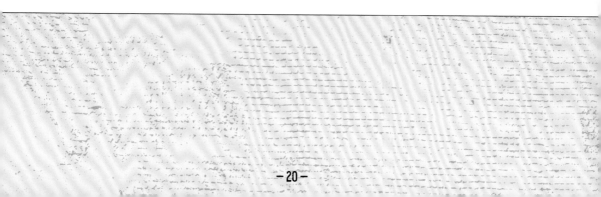

Some of the students who were part of the *Davis v. County School Board of Prince Edward County* lawsuit

The Black families of Prince Edward County were hopeful about change, but white people were angry. They took their anger out on Black families. They wanted to pressure Black people into stopping their fight against segregation. Teachers at Moton High School lost their jobs. White business owners fired Black employees. And many Black people were turned away from white stores where they used to shop freely.

People in the community knew Johns was one of the leaders in the effort to desegregate the schools. The Ku Klux Klan burned a cross at the school. And her father had heard about threatening comments white people had made about Johns. Her parents feared for her safety. They sent her to live with her uncle Vernon in Montgomery.

But the fight Johns had begun continued in the courts.

Montgomery, Alabama, in 1950

CHAPTER FIVE

THE HIGHEST COURT IN THE LAND

On March 7, 1952, judges **ruled** against the Black families in *Davis v. County School Board of Prince Edward County*. They did not **overturn** the state's law requiring school segregation. "We have found no hurt or harm to either race," they wrote.

The NAACP submitted an **appeal** to the Supreme Court. The Supreme Court combined the case with four other cases challenging school segregation. The combined cases were named *Brown v. Board of Education*. The NAACP argued its case before the Supreme Court in December 1952.

FACT The Supreme Court is the most powerful court in the United States. Their decisions can overrule decisions made by lower courts and previous Supreme Court decisions.

The U.S. Supreme Court building in Washington, DC

On May 17, 1954, the Supreme Court made a decision in *Brown v. Board of Education*. The justices decided that segregated schools were not equal at all. They outlawed segregation in public schools. Their ruling would also help end segregation in other spaces.

After the ruling, change didn't happen quickly in Prince Edward County. The school board actually shut down all of its schools in 1959. That way, they would not have to integrate. Five years later, in 1964, the Supreme Court forced the county to open the public schools again.

Black children enter Mary E. Branch Elementary School in Farmville in 1963. It was one of four local schools the federal government helped support after the county closed its public schools.

The Many Cases of
Brown v. Board of Education

Brown v. Board of Education is one of the most well-known legal cases in U.S. history. It was actually five cases challenging school segregation across the country—in Delaware, Kansas, South Carolina, Virginia, and Washington, DC. But we know it by just one case—*Brown v. Board of Education.*

Those five cases were part of an even larger legal strategy to end segregation that the NAACP had started in the 1930s. The ruling in the 1954 Supreme Court case was the result of decades of work by the NAACP. And it would take decades more to chip away at segregation in schools—and other spaces.

A sign recognizing the *Brown v. Board of Education* case in front of a school in Topeka, Kansas

CHAPTER SIX

A NEW START

Johns completed her last year of high school after moving to Montgomery, Alabama. Then, she enrolled in Spelman College. Just before Johns started college, she met William Holland Rowland Powell, a minister. They married in 1955 and had five children. Johns later finished her degree at Drexel University in 1979. She worked as a librarian for the Philadelphia public school system until her death in 1991.

In Farmville, the Robert Russa Moton Museum tells Johns's amazing story. The museum is housed in the Moton High School building. So Johns's story lives on where her fight for justice began.

Robert Russa Moton Museum

IT SEEMED LIKE REACHING FOR THE MOON.

BARBARA JOHNS

A sculpture honoring Johns's fight for a better school at the state capitol in Richmond, Virginia

FACT Recently, leaders in Virginia recognized Johns's legacy. A state office building in Richmond and the library in Farmville were renamed in her honor. There are also plans to place a sculpture of Johns at the U.S. Capitol in Washington, DC.

GLOSSARY

activist (AK-tuh-vist)—a person who works for social or political change

appeal (uh-PEEL)—a formal request to try a lawsuit again, in a higher court

integrate (IN-tuh-grate)—to bring people of different races together in schools and other public places

laboratory (LAB-ruh-tor-ee)—a room or building used for scientific experiments

overturn (oh-vur-TURN)—to make a legal decision no longer valid

racism (RAY-siz-uhm)—the belief that one race is better than another race

rule (ROOL)—to make a decision in a court case

segregation (seg-ruh-GAY-shuhn)—the practice of keeping groups of people apart, especially based on race

sever (SEV-ur)—to separate, as though you were cutting something

strike (STRIKE)—refusing to do something because of a disagreement about an action or the conditions of something

superintendent (soo-pur-in-TEN-duhnt)—a person who directs or manages an organization, such as a school district

READ MORE

Armand, Glenda. *Black Leaders in the Civil Rights Movement: A Black History Book for Kids.* Emeryville, CA: Rockridge Press, 2021.

Tyner, Artika R. *The Untold Story of Sarah Keys Evans: Civil Rights Soldier.* North Mankato, MN: Capstone, 2023.

Weston, Margeaux. *Brown v. Board of Education: A Day That Changed America.* North Mankato, MN: Capstone, 2022.

INTERNET SITES

National Geographic Kids: The Road to School Desegregation
kids.nationalgeographic.com/history/article/the-road-to-school-desegregation

National Geographic Kids: Thurgood Marshall
kids.nationalgeographic.com/history/article/thurgood-marshall

National Women's Hall of Fame: Barbara Rose Johns Powell
womenofthehall.org/inductee/barbara-rose-johns-powell

INDEX

ABOUT THE AUTHOR

Nicole A. Mansfield is an African American author and a mother of three. She is married to her Italian American husband. Between the two of them, they speak four different languages! She has lived in four different countries and 13 different cities around the world! Nicole cares deeply about faith, family, culture, and history. She wants the children of today to learn more about true stories of the past!